August 1967

"HISTORY OF THE MK 25 WARHEAD (U)"

SC-M-67-663

Weapon Systems

Redacted Version

Information Research Division, 3434

SC-M-67-663

12

RESTRICTED DATA

This document contains restricted data as defined in the Atomic Energy Act of 1954. Its transmittal or the disclosure of its contents in any manner to an unauthorized person is prohibited.

THIS DOCUMENT CONSISTS OF ___32___ PAGES

F-101B aircraft with GENIE rocket

KS 5454/12

(b)(1), (b)(3)

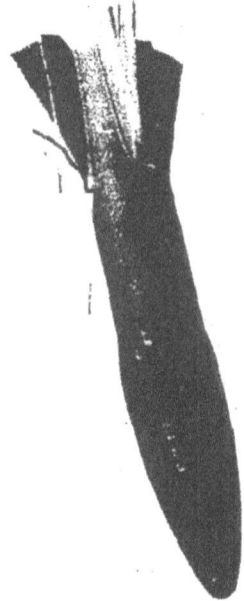

(b)(1), (b)(3)

MK 25 MOD 0

Figure 3. MK 25 Cross Section

SECRET

RESTRICTED DATA

Timetable of Mk 25 Warhead Events

3/13/51   Division of Military Application proposes that nuclear warheads be used for defense against mass aircraft raids.

2/27/52   Joint Chiefs of Staff request Joint Air Defense Board to prepare a staff study.

1/14/53   Joint Air Defense Board publishes staff study.

4/28/54

(b)(1), (b)(3)

5/7/54   Atomic Energy Commission accepts responsibility for developing a warhead for the air-to-air rocket.

5/18/54

(b)(1), (b)(3)

6/4/54   Warhead assigned designation of XW-25.

8/9/54   Joint Study Group considers details of XW-25 design.

9/22/54

(b)(1), (b)(3)

3/17/55   Assistant Secretary of Defense authorizes full development of XW-25 rocket/warhead project.

Spring 1955

(b)(1), (b)(3)

3/30/55   Military Liaison Committee requests that warheads be produced by January 1, 1957.

6/9/55   Division of Military Application requests emergency capability program.

8/24/55   Proposed ordnance characteristics report presented to Special Weapons Development Board and accepted.

(b)(3)

RESTRICTED DATA

SECRET

(b)(1), (b)(3)

7/56	Mk 25 Mod 0 Warhead design released.
12/56	Emergency capability units produced.
2/20/57	Design release report presented to Special Weapons Development Board and accepted.
6/57	Mk 25 Mod 0 Warhead enters stockpile.

(b)(1), (b)(3)

10/61	Mk 25 Mod 1 Warhead, with environmental sensing device, design released.
3/62	Mk 25 Mod 1 Warhead enters stockpile.

Atomic Demolition Munition

10/28/53	Joint Chiefs of Staff recommend development of a lightweight atomic demolition munition.
4/2/54	Military-Liaison Committee releases military characteristics for the munition.
2/56	Mk 25 munition application canceled.

HONEST JOHN, JR.

9/28/54	Assistant Secretary of Defense requests Atomic Energy Commission to assist in studies of a short-range HONEST JOHN weapons system.
4/27/55	Division of Military Application proposes set of military characteristics for the HONEST JOHN, JR. adaption kit.
2/28/56	Division of Military Application cancels project.

Boosted XW-25 Warhead

7/13/56	Division of Military Application suggests development of boosted XW-25 Warhead.

8/14/56   Study of boosted warhead released. GENIE warhead compart-
            ment too small.

9/14/56

(b)(1), (b)(3)

5/27/57   Assistant Secretary of Defense requests Atomic Energy Com-
            mission to conduct feasibility study of a warhead to
            minimize plutonium hazards of defense rockets.

7/22/57

(b)(1), (b)(3)

11/27/57   Military requirement for boosted XW-25 Warhead canceled.

RESTRICTED DATA

History of the Mk 25 Warhead

As the weight of nuclear devices began to shrink and their yields to increase, it became apparent that many types of aircraft and missiles could be fitted with nuclear or thermonuclear warheads, making it at least theoretically possible for a potential enemy to saturate the defenses of the United States with a single massive attack. A system which destroyed a reasonable percentage of the attacking bombers would provide adequate defense against conventional bombs, but a relatively small number of well-placed atomic weapons could do much toward destroying an industrial complex.

There was no competent defense against such an attack; in fact, there was not even an adequate counter to the V-2 missile used by the Germans in World War II. Enemy air bases and launching sites could be destroyed, and the Strategic Air Command had assigned high priority to these targets. However, since the national policy was not to strike first, it was obvious that the country would have to be prepared to absorb the initial brunt of an all-out attack by an aggressor.[1] The Division of Military Application accordingly suggested, March 13, 1951, that some thought be given to providing a nuclear warhead to be used as a weapon of defense against mass aircraft raids.[2] Little immediate action was taken, however, since the existing state-of-the-art, both in warheads capable of high-altitude operation, and in missiles capable of achieving such altitudes with the requisite accuracy, was not sufficiently advanced.

As the capabilities of both warheads and missiles increased, the Joint Chiefs of Staff, February 27, 1952, requested their Joint Air Defense Board to study the situation. This study took place during much of 1952 and, October 29, 1952, the Military Liaison Committee notified the Division of Military Application that it was entirely possible that a

RESTRICTED DATA

military requirement for one or more specific weapons for air defense
would be forthcoming in the near future. It was requested that the
atomic Energy Commission undertake preliminary investigation of the
problems involved in developing air defense atomic warheads, with par-
ticular reference to the ability of such warheads to operate at high
altitudes.[3]

The Joint Air Defense Board completed its study and released a report
January 14, 1953. This report listed the various potential carriers for
atomic devices, such as guns, rockets, missiles, interceptor and bomber
aircraft, and recommended the use of ground-to-air missiles such as the
TALOS, BOMARC and NIKE, which would carry low yield, highly economical,
and efficient nuclear warheads.[1]

The report was discussed in the January 12, 1953, meeting of the Special
Weapons Development Board. It was predicted that air defense warheads
would have to be produced in large numbers, possibly tens of thousands,
in order to provide an effective defense of any sizable portion of the
country. They would thus have to be economical, both in nuclear and nonnuclear costs. These weapons would have to be operationally ready at all
times to respond to a surprise attack, and they would have to be able to
withstand exposure to climatic extremes ranging from the arctic to the
tropics. The weapons should require only minor maintenance, since it
would not be possible to provide a sufficiently large group of thoroughly
trained technicians.

The Air Force BOMARC was being designed for an extended perimeter defense
which would use a long-range detection system, also being developed. The
range of this detection system was from 250 to 300 miles. The BOMARC
range would be 125 miles, initially, with a later extension to 250 miles.
The early altitude capability would be 60,000 feet, and this would be
increased to 100,000 feet as enemy capabilities increased. Since BOMARC
would not be operational until 1959 or 1960, a Navy missile, the TALOS-W,
was planned for interim use, and would be available about 2 years before

BOMARC. The NIKE-B was an Army missile to be used in conjunction with NIKE I nonnuclear tactical units. Its range was relatively short, about 50 miles.

(b)(1), (b)(3)

The Air Force was also planning another antiaircraft weapon, a high-velocity air-to-air rocket which would deliver an atomic warhead. This would be carried on interceptors, and such manned aircraft would help identify suspicious vehicles. Since any air-defense detection system would have to operate under peacetime conditions, it was felt that the decision whether unidentified aircraft were friendly or not should be made under human control.[4]

Sandia notified the Santa Fe Operations Office, August 18, 1953, that an investigation of air defense warhead designs had been under way since late 1952. Consideration had been given to the possible deleterious effects of high altitudes on weapon operation. The effects of cosmic activity, ion concentration, and the presence of ozone had been investigated, but it appeared that high voltage breakdown under conditions of reduced atmospheric pressure was the only problem of real concern. Existing firing sets were unsuitable for such operation, and design improvements were being studied on such items as detonators, X-units and cabling.[5]

The TX-N Committee discussed the air defense warhead program in a meeting August 25, 1953, and proposed that a canned or sealed capsule be designed for operation at high altitudes. For an immediate solution, it was suggested that the warhead compartment be provided with a continuous supply of dried air, which would increase the internal pressure and thus deter electrical arcing, and also help to prevent corrosion.[6]

Previously, there had been a strong tendency on the part of the Military to encourage standardization of nuclear and nonnuclear weapon components. This trend was to some extent reversed in the case of air defense warheads,

UNCLASSIFIED

RS 3434/12

as it was felt that these weapons had to be specialized in order to provide an immediate readiness capability, maximum economy in the use of
fissionable material, and a high degree of reliability against premature
detonation. Such direction was provided in a letter from Field Command
to Sandia dated October 15, 1953, and eventually several air defense
warhead designs were produced, the Mks 25, 30 and 31.[7]

(b)(1), (b)(3)

At the request of the TX-N Committee, Sandia studied the optimum size
for warheads for air-to-air use.

(b)(1), (b)(3)

The Atomic Energy Commission wrote to the Military Liaison Committee May 7,
1954, accepting responsibility for the development of a warhead for the
air-to-air rocket.

(b)(1), (b)(3)

Field Command released a set of approved military characteristics for a
15-inch warhead May 18, 1954.

(b)(1), (b)(3)

The warhead would be
capable of remaining in a ready-to-fire condition for a period of at least
30 days. It would be able to withstand, without damage, single mission

UNCLASSIFIED

flights of 2 hours and a total flight duration of 50 hours at altitudes up to 100,000 feet and subject to temperatures ranging from -90°F to +165°F. Resistance to accelerations of ±100 g's along the longitudinal axis, ±20 g's along any perpendicular axis, and angular accelerations of 400 radians/second/second would be required. The firing system would be able to operate to an altitude of 100,000 feet.[11]

At the request of the TX-N Committee,[12] the designation XW-25 was assigned to the warhead June 4, 1954.[13] The Division of Military Application noted that the Air Force would be responsible for the ballistic case, arming and fuzing system, power supply, propulsion system, and associated assembly, test and handling equipment. The Atomic Energy Commission would provide the implosion warhead, including nuclear capsule, pit, high-explosive system, detonators, cables, X-unit, firing switch, nuclear insertion gear, sphere case, and associated assembly, test and handling equipment.[14]

The missile was given the code name of DING DONG, and a Joint Study Group named, with representatives from the Air Force Special Weapons Center, Armed Forces Special Weapons Project, Los Alamos, and Sandia, and this group initially met August 9, 1954. The weapon would be optimized for the F-102 interceptor, with secondary applications to the F-86, F-89 and F-100 aircraft. The Air Force Special Weapons Center was assigned overall responsibility for the weapon system, with the assistance of Wright Air Development Center.

The outer diameter of DING DONG, exclusive of fins, would be about 16.5 inches, but excursions to 15 and 18 inches would be investigated to determine their influence on performance. The total length of the weapon would be compatible with the launching restrictions of the applicable bomb bays. The use of both fixed and folding fins would be considered. If a reversible actuating mechanism for fin extension and retraction was provided, it would be capable of repeated operation while the weapon was being externally carried at air speeds up to 250 knots. If an automatic,

RS 3434/12

one-time fin operating device was used, its probability of operational failure was not to be greater than 1 in 10,000. This mechanism would have to operate at speeds up to Mach 1.5 and at altitudes up to 35,000 feet.

There would be three sequential signals required to detonate the warhead; one to actuate the nuclear arming mechanism, another to initiate electrical arming, and a third to provide the firing signals. The fuze would include a safe-separation feature to prevent premature warhead detonation. A detonation timing element, capable of being preset before aircraft takeoff, would be designed. The rocket would have a 2500 feet per second (1700 miles per hour) velocity increase over its aircraft speed and a flight time of 15 seconds to target. The weapon would be used tactically at all altitudes up to 50,000 feet.[15]

(b)(1), (b)(3)

A study of kill versus yield was made by the Joint Study Group, and published November 30, 1954.

(b)(1), (b)(3)

With the larger weapons, the launching range had to be increased to provide enough escape time. This increase in range decreased the probability of target detection, and more than offset any increase in effectiveness.

(b)(1), (b)(3)

In respect to the warhead diameter, the cost per kill in terms of nuclear material was less in the largest diameter studied, which was 18 inches. However, larger diameters would require corresponding increases in the size and weight of the carrying rocket and would cause aircraft compatibility problems. The recommended diameter was 17.25 inches.

(b)(1), (b)(3)

The study indicated that it would be desirable to provide a missile velocity increase of 3000 feet per second during the rocket flight and, since missile contractors had indicated that this would be possible, it was recommended that the rocket and warhead be designed to this specification.

The design criteria required that the warhead be considerably different than previous designs. It must be able to withstand 100 g's, it must be light so as to attain high velocity, it must be capable of being carried at high altitudes for many hours and still operate, and it must be capable of withstanding the very high temperatures generated in high speed flight.[17]

The Joint Study Group was later dissolved and reconstituted as the Air-to-Air Rocket Joint Project Group, and held its first meeting under the new title January 31, 1955. The warhead weight, by the latest estimate, was about 230 pounds, and Douglas Aircraft Company, which was to provide the rocket, was requested to design to this figure. The Group recommended that the warhead thermal battery be made an integral part of the X-unit and sealed into this package. An arm/safe switch, capable of being monitored, and located in the X-unit charging circuit, would be operated either automatically or manually.[18]

The Assistant Secretary of Defense, March 17, 1955, authorized full development activities on Project DING DONG. The Armed Forces Special Weapons Project would have normal responsibilities, but the Air Force would possess overriding authority within the Department of Defense during the development period.[19]

Sandia notified Santa Fe Operations Office March 18, 1955, that the Military had indicated an urgent desire to have the DING DONG weapon operational by 1957. Since this meant that an appreciable number of weapons would have to be available at that time, it was requested that an authorization for quantity production be released.[20] The Atomic Energy Commission replied that since no firm production directive for the XW-25 Warhead had been received, it was premature to authorize production.[21]

(b)(1), (b)(3)

(b)(1), (b)(3)

The Military Liaison Committee wrote to the Atomic Energy Commission March 30, 1955, requesting that the small atomic warhead be developed in time to match a predicted rocket availability date of January 1, 1957. This required that the warhead be ready for operational suitability tests by July 1, 1956. It was noted that feasibility studies were being made of this warhead for use in other applications, such as a demolition munition, but these studies were not to interfere with the urgent need for the air-to-air capability.

The warhead would be rugged, reliable, and easily installed and tested; it would be safe to transport and handle; and easy to use in combat. It would provide maximum interchangeability of nonnuclear components between it and other atomic warheads, although this requirement was not to preclude development of a sealed design.

(b)(1), (b)(3)

The diameter of the warhead would be 17-1/4 inches, and the weight and length would be held to a minimum.

The warhead installed in a weapon would be capable of storage in the ready-to-operate condition for a period of at least 30 days, but extension of this time to 90 days was desired if it could be attained on a not-to-delay basis. The warhead would be operable at altitudes up to 75,000 feet, with 100,000 feet as an ultimate goal. It would withstand temperatures and accelerations specified in the military characteristics.

(b)(1), (b)(3)

Santa Fe Operations Office notified the Division of Military Application April 15, 1955, that Sandia was planning system flight tests of the XW-25 between November 1955 and August 1956, warhead design release in March 1956, and early Mark-quality units delivered to War Reserve by mid-1957. This schedule could be accelerated if flight test rockets could be provided at an earlier date.[24]

Some concern had been felt over incorporating thermal batteries in the warhead. It was felt that this prevented nuclear safing, allowed components essential for full-scale nuclear detonation to be continuously present, and permitted the squibs of the batteries to be initiated by fire or any external radio frequency device. A careful evaluation was made and a report issued April 28, 1955, which described several methods of safing. These included removal of the batteries from the warhead, a safety device in the battery circuit, a thermally-operated switch to open the circuit in the event of fire, late arming switches in the high-voltage circuits, or an arm/safe switch in the warhead or adaption kit.

The first two methods would not contribute to the safety of the overall weapon. The thermally-operated switch would protect against only one type of failure. Late arming switches would have to be low-energy devices, and would be heat-sensitive. The arm/safe switch was thus selected for use. If this was located in the adaption kit, a high-voltage line would have to be extended from the sealed warhead compartment to the adaption kit. However, if the switch was placed in the warhead, it would be protected by the warhead seal and could be placed on the high side of the X-unit where it could also be used to short out the battery or capacitor and improve the safety margin. This switch would be actuated automatically, to guard against any possible degradation in reliability due to pilot error.[25]

The Air Force issued a report on the arming and fuzing system for the air-to-air rocket April 28, 1955. Three systems had been analyzed, and it was concluded that one with an arming plug and a monitored switch in the warhead would have the least probability of premature detonation during storage. It was also concluded that protection against premature detonation before safe separation would be adequate if a thermal switch was provided.[26]

(b)(1), (b)(3)

Since high volume warhead production was anticipated, it was planned to delay production until much of the developmental and operational testing had been completed, in order to prevent any extensive retrofit. Thus Mark-quality warheads would not become available in quantity until September 1957.[27]

The Military Liaison Committee replied, May 19, 1955, that rocket development had been committed to a capability date of January 1, 1957. Initial application would be to 25 modified F-89 aircraft (which had replaced the F-102 due to a delay in the latter airplane), and which were to be available by late 1956.

(b)(3)

The DING DONG rocket design now began to take final shape, and was described in a letter from Field Command May 24, 1955. This unguided rocket would have a range from 3 to 5 miles, with an average incremental velocity of 3000 feet per second over its launch speed. The rocket could operate at altitudes up to 60,000 feet, but would be limited by interceptor performance, safe-escape range, radar detection angles, and angle of attack.

The overall length of the rocket (including warhead assembly) would be 114 inches, its maximum outside diameter, exclusive of fins, 17.25 inches, and its gross weight 807 pounds. The diameter with fins retracted would be 22 inches, and with fins extended 34 inches. The weapon would be a comparatively simple assembly consisting of a solid-propellant rocket motor, pressure-sealed warhead, and a nose cone of approximately 2.5 fineness ratio containing an encapsulated fuzing and firing system. External carriage on the F-89 and internal carriage in the F-102 would be provided, with secondary capabilities on any Air Force and Navy fighter aircraft that proved operationally suitable.[29]

The Division of Military Application notified Santa Fe Operations Office June 9, 1955, that the Air Force was accelerating the rocket flight-test schedule, and requested that warhead time scales be similarly advanced.

(b)(3)

This effort would be kept separate from the XW-25 production program and the units would be suitable only for short-term operational employment. No production engineering would be done, the weapons were not to be of Mark quality, and would be retired as soon as regular Mark 25 production permitted.[30]

(b)(3)

Los Alamos would make an earlier release to the AEC production system, and Sandia would provide the necessary components by extension of development orders. It was noted that the most critical warhead component would be the high-voltage arm/safe switch. This component was the first of its type, and had severe size limitations and high acceleration requirements.[31]

Report SC3682(TR), Proposed Ordnance Characteristics of the XW-25 Warhead for the Air-to-Air Rocket, was discussed in the August 24, 1955, meeting of the Special Weapons Development Board. The weapon had a rocket-motor thrust of 36,250 pounds. The folding sections of the rocket fins were retracted into the fixed section by aircraft control and extended by individual pneumatic cylinders, which were activated after launch by rocket motor pressure. Two umbilical connectors were provided between rocket and carrying aircraft. One contained wires leading to the warhead adaption kit, and the other to the rocket motor ignitor. The two connectors were used to prevent running wires through the sealed portion of the warhead.

The primary aircraft carrier would be the F-102, which would be operationally available in late 1957. Since the intercept problem was complex, the pilot used an automatic fire-control system to launch the missile. This control system detected the target, provided course steering information to the aircraft pilot, and launched the weapon in accordance with a predetermined fuze setting.

(b)(3)

'The nuclear system was hermetically sealed, thus eliminating corrosion problems.

The only handling equipment required for the warhead was a shipping container. Two testers would be provided; one to check the integrity of the warhead seal, and the other to test continuity in the thermal battery initiation circuit and monitor the position of the arm/safe battery switch. Since use of the weapon might be required at short notice, no preflight testing would be necessary. Periodic checks would, however, be made, ranging from a 30-day pressure seal check to an 18-month teardown to check the effects of aging on interior components.

Design release of the warhead was scheduled for July 1956, and a number of production units would be delivered by June 1957. The report was accepted by the Board and forwarded to the Division of Military Application.[32]

(b)(1), (b)(3)

(b)(1), (b)(3)

Sandia suggested, in a letter to Santa Fe Operations Office June 5, 1956, that the production warhead resulting from the XW-25 program be called the Mk 25 Mod 0 Warhead, abbreviated W25-0.

(b)(3)

The production nomenclature was accepted by the AEC June 26, 1956, but the preproduction items were labeled EC-25 Warheads, to distinguish them from development warheads.[34]

(b)(1), (b)(3)

No other completely satisfactory switch was available, and much modification of the warhead, rocket fuze, and aircraft fire-control system would have been required if another switch were substituted. Thus the EC-25 Warheads did not contain this switch.[36]

Report SC3932(TR), Status Report at Design Release of the Mk 25 Mod 0 Warhead, was presented to and accepted by the February 20, 1957, meeting of the Special Weapons Development Board. This noted that the warhead had been developed for use in the Air Force air-to-air rocket GENIE (a change of name for the DING DONG), which was designed to operate from

UNCLASSIFIED

RS 3434/12

sea level to 60,000 feet, with flight times (depending on altitude) of 5-1/2 to 12 seconds, and which were determined by the requirements for safe separation from the delivery aircraft. The GENIE weighed 800 pounds, was 115 inches long, and 17.5 inches in diameter.[37]

The Mk 25 Mod 0 Warhead had been design-released in July 1956, and stock-pile entry effected in June 1957. The emergency capability units were <u>completed</u> on schedule.

(b)(1), (b)(3)

The warhead was sealed and pressurized to 15 pounds per square inch on assembly, to prevent arc-over of high voltages at high altitudes. Capability was established with the F-89 aircraft, with later application to the F-101 and F-106 as these became available.

Operation of the weapon was as follows: A ground-control center located an approaching enemy aircraft and directed the interceptor to it. The target was located on the interceptor's fire-control system, which provided attack information to the pilot. After the pilot switched to the special weapons option and the radar locked-on to the target, the fire-control system operated the arm/safe switch to the arm position. Subsequently, a capacitor used to fire the low-voltage thermal batteries in the fuze was charged and a timing signal issued.

The weapon was launched automatically by the fire-control system when the interceptor entered the correct position at the proper range, which was dictated primarily by radiation safety considerations. At launch, an acceleration switch opened and inertial switches closed and latched to fire low-voltage thermal batteries. The timer then started to operate. At burnout, about 2 seconds after launch, the acceleration switch closed, firing the warhead high-voltage thermal batteries, and charging the warhead capacitors. When the timer completed its rundown, the weapon detonated. If the target was lost before launch, the arm/safe switch automatically returned to the safe position, and it could be subsequently rearmed or resafed as many times as necessary.

The successful completion of the program was greeted with enthusiasm by the Air Force, and Sandia was complimented on its part of the work.[38] The W25-0 was hailed as the first of a group of weapons that would require little inspection and would be called "wooden bombs," so termed because it was hoped their maintenance would be only that of a block of pine.

(b)(1), (b)(3)

Report SC4190(TR), Engineering Evaluation of the Mk 25 Mod 0 Warhead, was issued August 1958. The system environmental and initial flight test program had been successfully completed. Flight tests had proven compatibility of the warhead with the MB-1 or GENIE rocket, and resulted in certification of the F-89 aircraft as a carrier. Flight tests were continuing to prove compatibility of the weapon system with F-101 and F-106 aircraft.

A series of seven airdrop and five sled tests had shown that a charged X-unit would not discharge upon impact unless a firing signal had been received by the fuze, but that an armed fuze would probably fire. Thus, the probability of a nuclear detonation was high if a GENIE struck the ground with an armed fuze and X-unit. However, the probability of an air dud in such cases was low, since the primary cause of an air dud was an arming failure.[39]

The Division of Military Application authorized the installation of environmental sensing devices in the Mk 25 Warhead, and this information was furnished to Sandia by the Albuquerque Operations Office January 30, 1961.[40] Sandia subsequently designed the Mk 25 Mod 1 Warhead which was released October 1961 and entered stockpile March 1962. This change provided an inertial switch which was installed in the high-voltage battery activation circuit of the X-unit and prevented inadvertent operation of the warhead firing set until the warhead had experienced a launch acceleration.[41]

Atomic Demolition Munition

The Joint Chiefs of Staff recommended to the Secretary of Defense, October 28, 1953, that a lightweight atomic demolition munition be developed. On November 3, 1953, the Assistant Secretary of Defense requested that the Armed Forces Special Weapons Project coordinate a statement of suitable military characteristics for such a warhead 15 inches in diameter, 30 inches in length, and weight not over 200 pounds.

(b)(1), (b)(3)

The weapon would have a readiness period of 30 days, and be capable of disassembly into 40-pound packages.[42]

(b)(1), (b)(3)

Little work was done on the project, however, and the application was canceled in February 1956 in favor of similar devices on the Mk 30 and Mk 31 programs.[44]

HONEST JOHN, JR.

The Assistant Secretary of Defense notified the Atomic Energy Commission September 28, 1954, that the Army had initiated studies of an HONEST JOHN, JR., or short-range HONEST JOHN, weapons system, and wished to include an atomic capability with the XW-25 Warhead. It was requested that the AEC help in the project, but not to interfere with the high-priority development of the air-to-air application of this warhead.[45]

The proposed military characteristics for an adaption kit for this system
were released by the Division of Military Application April 27, 1955.[46]
These called for a small, implosion-type atomic warhead with a diameter
from 15 to 17 inches. The weapon would be a surface-to-surface rocket
fired from two types of launchers; a self-propelled and a lightweight
helicopter-transportable version.

(b)(3)

The fuzing system would provide a sig-
nal to the warhead after a preset time had elapsed and a preset velocity
had been attained. Again, little work was accomplished, and on February 28,
1956, the Division of Military Application notified Santa Fe Operations
Office that the Army had discontinued plans for the above application,
in favor of a warhead with a higher yield and small diameter.[44]

Boosted XW-25 Warhead

The Division of Military Application, July 13, 1956, noted that the Department of Defense had informally expressed concern about the lack of
a boosted XW-25 Warhead.[47] Albuquerque Operations Office replied, in a
teletype of July 25, 1956, that no formal interest in such a warhead had
ever been stated, nor had the Laboratories been requested to undertake
this development. The need for such a warhead was questioned, and it was
requested that information be supplied as to whether this was due to a
desire for nuclear economy, higher yield, or concern about plutonium
contamination.[48]

The Division of Military Application responded, July 30, 1956, noting
that the military request resulted from a study prepared at the request
of the Joint Chiefs of Staff.

(b)(1), (b)(3)

RESTRICTED DATA

This study was released August 14, 1956. It was noted that the GENIE rocket warhead compartment was not large enough to accommodate boosting equipment and that the development of a suitable system would result in an entirely new weapon design.[59]

(b)(1), (b)(3)

The Division of Military Application wrote to Los Alamos September 14, 1956, noting that a possible plutonium hazard would be created by the XW-25 when making peacetime intercepts of unidentified aircraft. Additionally, the Air Force had requested that a study be made of the feasibility of producing warheads containing only uranium-235, to reduce the hazards to civilian populations and air bases from contamination caused by one-point detonations or fire.

(b)(1), (b)(3)

A Joint Feasibility Group was convened, which reported November 9, 1956. This Group had examined several different types of nuclear designs, and noted that an implosion warhead containing only uranium-235 would ease the contamination problem, but that complete elimination would be possible only through use of a gun-type design. Radiological contamination was currently of much interest, and attempts were being made to minimize the hazards associated with the transportation, storage and use of atomic weapons.[53]

Subsequently, May 27, 1957, the Assistant Secretary of Defense directed the Atomic Energy Commission to cooperate with the Armed Forces Special Weapons Project and the Services in a feasibility study of an atomic warhead that would minimize the plutonium hazard of defense rockets. without unduly increasing the nuclear material costs.[54]

(b)(1), (b)(3)

RESTRICTED DATA

UNCLASSIFIED

SECRET

RS 3434/12

(b)(1), (b)(3)

UNCLASSIFIED

RS 3434/12

Glossary of Mk 25 Terms

Adaption Kit -- Those items peculiar to the warhead installion less the warhead.

Air Force Special Weapons Center -- That element of the Air Force Systems Command having to do with compatibility testing of nuclear devices with aircraft. Located at Kirtland Air Force Base, New Mexico.

Albuquerque Operations Office -- Change of name for the Santa Fe Operations Office, effective April 2, 1956.

Armed Forces Special Weapons Project -- An interdepartmental agency formed to handle military functions related to atomic weapons.

Arming -- The act of arming a weapon; that is, preparing it for firing.

Assistant Secretary of Defense -- Created by Department of Defense directive, June 30, 1953, as part of DOD reorganization. Handles research and development activities of the DOD.

Atomic Demolition Munition -- An atomic device capable of being manually carried and emplaced for detonation.

Boosted Weapon -- A weapon to which deuterium and tritium gas has been added to produce an increase in fissioning and, consequently, yield.

Bureau of Ordnance -- That part of the Navy Department having to do with design and procurement of ordnance.

(b)(1), (b)(3)

Department of Defense -- The Armed Forces; i.e., the Army, Navy and Air Force.

Detonators -- Devices containing bridge wires which, when subjected to an electrical current, burn rapidly and act as a match to apply a flame to various points on the outer surface of the high-explosive sphere.

Explosive device which when initiated by the x-unit ignite the lense charges of the high explosive sphere.

UNCLASSIFIED

UNCLASSIFIED

RS 3434/12

Division of Military Application -- An AEC office that functions as liaison between the Military and weapons designers and producers.

(b)(1), (b)(3)

Field Command -- The local office of the Armed Forces Special Weapons Project, located on Sandia Base, Albuquerque, New Mexico.

Firing System -- The electrical system of the weapon that produces and applies a high voltage current to the detonators.

Fuze -- A combination of the arming and firing devices of a weapon.

Fuzing System -- The system that ~~signals the start of high voltage charging of the firing system~~ *arms the weapon at the appropriate time and provides a firing signal to the firing system at the selected burst height*

g -- Force equal to one unit gravity.

Gas Boosting -- The technique of increasing the yield of a nuclear device by introducing deuterium-tritium gas into the implosion process to increase the fission activity.

Gun-Type Design -- An atomic weapon based on the principle that a supercritical mass of nuclear material can be created by bringing together two subcritical masses of such material.

High-Explosive Sphere -- The ball of high explosive that surrounds the nuclear ~~primary and~~ *fissionable capsule and is designed to* produce the implosion effect when detonated.

Implosion -- The effect created when a sphere of high explosive is detonated on its exterior surface. *provides with appropriate lens charges to direct the explosion* The force of the shock wave is directed largely toward the center of the sphere.

Initiator -- A source of neutrons.

UNCLASSIFIED

Joint Chiefs of Staff -- An Army, Navy, Air Force group to determine policy and to develop joint strategic objectives of the Armed Forces.

Kilogram -- A metric weight approximating 2.2 pounds.

Kiloton -- A means of measuring the yield of an atomic device by comparing its output with the effect of an explosion of TNT. A 1-kiloton yield is equivalent to the detonation effect of 1000 tons of high explosive.

Los Alamos Scientific Laboratory -- A nuclear design organization located at Los Alamos, New Mexico.

Mach -- A measure of speed. Mach 1.0 is the speed of sound, or 738 miles per hour at sea level.

Mark Quality -- A quality high enough for stockpile acceptance.

Military Characteristics -- The attributes of a weapon that are desired by the Military.

Military Liaison Committee -- A Department of Defense committee established by the Atomic Energy Act to advise and consult with the AEC on all matters relating to military applications of atomic energy.

Missile Warhead -- The explosive or nuclear device carried by a missile.

(b)(1), (b)(3)

(b)(1), (b)(3)

Safe-Separation Time -- A time interval provided by a timer to allow safe escape of an aircraft delivering a weapon before the weapon detonates.

Safing -- Putting a weapon in condition such that it cannot fire.

Santa Fe Operations Office -- The local office of the Atomic Energy Commission (AEC) concerned with the Sandia operations.

Sealed Pit -- A weapon in which all the nuclear components (except the boosting gas, when used) are permanently installed in place. Designed to eliminate the need for inflight nuclear insertion mechanisms.

Services -- The Department of Defense.

Special Weapons Development Board -- A joint Sandia-Military board at Sandia Base to provide local guidance on weapons design.

Squib -- A device containing a small powder charge. When detonated, the resulting gas pressure closes a switch or performs a similar action. A light, quick-acting, one-shot device.

Strategic Air Command -- A part of the United States Air Force devoted to the attack of strategic targets, such as industrial plants.

Teapot -- A less-than-full-scale test series held at the Nevada Test Site. Series of 14 tests, starting February 18 and ending May 15, 1955.

Thermal Battery -- A battery whose electrolyte is in a solid state while inactive. To activate, heat is applied to this electrolyte, melting it and putting the battery into active output condition.

Thermonuclear -- Two-stage reaction, with a fission device exploding and starting a fusion reaction in light elements.

~~SECRET~~
-32-
~~RESTRICTED DATA~~

Tritium -- The hydrogen isotope of mass number 3.

Two-Stage -- Combination of fission and fusion action in a weapon.

TX-N Committee -- A joint committee of Los Alamos Scientific Laboratory and Sandia members, established to guide the development of implosion-type weapons.

Uranium-235 -- A radioactive element, an isotope of uranium-238.

Uranium-238 -- A radioactive element, atomic number 92. Natural uranium contains about 99.3 percent uranium-238; the rest is uranium-235.

Warhead -- A weapon carried to the target by missile.

Wooden Bomb -- A weapon designed to have an infinite shelf life and to require no special storage or surveillance. "As trouble-free as a block of pine."

X-Unit -- ~~A high-voltage transformer.~~ A device used to provide high voltage to the weapon detonators.

References

1. SRD Minutes, RS 3466/79850, Special Weapons Development Board to Distribution, dtd 4/28/54, subject, Minutes of 82nd Meeting. SC Archives, Transfer No. 48217.

2. SRD Ltr, Division of Military Application to Santa Fe Operations Office, dtd 3/13/51, subject, Air-Launched Atomic Rocket. AEC Files, MRA-5, Vol II, 10/50-6/51.

3. SRD Ltr, RS 3466/67540, Military Liaison Committee to Division of Military Application, dtd 10/29/52, subject, Development of Atomic Weapons for Use in Air Defense. SC Central Technical Files, D-5, 1949-54.

4. SRD Minutes, RS 3466/84055, Special Weapons Development Board to Distribution, dtd 1/12/53, subject, Minutes of 89th Meeting. SC Archives, Transfer No. 48217.

5. SRD Ltr, RS 1000/1387, Sandia Corporation to Santa Fe Operations Office, dtd 8/18/53, subject, Preliminary Investigation of Problems Incident to Development of Atomic Weapons for Use in Air Defense. SC Central Technical Files, D-5, 1949-54.

6. SRD Ltr, RS 5000/92, TX-N Committee to Los Alamos Scientific Laboratory and Sandia Corporation, dtd 8/25/53, subject, Readiness Storage of Warheads and Nuclear Components. AEC Files, MRA-5, 7/53-8/53.

7. SRD Ltr, RS 3466/79235, Field Command to Sandia Corporation, dtd 10/15/53, subject, New Type Atomic Warheads for Air Defense. SC Central Technical Files, D-5, 1949-54.

8.

9.

(b)(1), (b)(3)

10.

11. SRD Ltr, Field Command to Distribution, dtd 5/18/54, subject, Transmittal of Military Characteristics. AEC Files, MRA-5, 5/54-6/54.

12. CRD Ltr, TX-N Steering Committee to Sandia Corporation, dtd 5/19/54, subject, XW-25. SC Central Technical Files, XW-25, 1954-61.

13. CRD Ltr, RS 1000/1577, Sandia Corporation to Santa Fe Operations Office, dtd 6/4/54, subject, Assignment of Development Nomenclature-- XW-25. SC Central Technical Files, XW-25, 1954-61.

14. SRD Ltr, Division of Military Application to Santa Fe Operations Office, dtd 5/19/54, subject, Proposed Division of Responsibilities for Development of an Atomic Warhead Air-to-Air Rocket. AEC Files, MRA-5, 5/54-6/54.

15. SRD Ltr, RS 3466/80037, Air Force Special Weapons Center to Sandia Corporation, dtd 8/17/54, subject, Meeting of Project DING DONG Study Group. SC Central Technical Files, XW-25, 1954-61.

16.

(b)(3)

17. SRD Report, Joint Study Group to Distribution, dtd 11/30/54, subject, Study of Kill versus Yield. SC Central Technical Files, XW-25, 1954-61.

18. SRD Report, Air-to-Air Rocket Joint Project Group to Distribution, dtd 1/31/55, subject, First Report. SC Central Technical Files, XW-25, 1954-61.

19. SRD Ltr, Assistant Secretary of Defense to United States Atomic Energy Commission, dtd 3/17/55. AEC Files, MRA-5, 10/54-6/55.

20. SRD Ltr, RS 1/696, Sandia Corporation to Santa Fe Operations Office, dtd 3/18/55, subject, XW-25 Program for Air-to-Air Rocket. SC Central Technical Files, XW-25, 1954-61.

21. SRD Ltr, Division of Military Application to Santa Fe Operations Office, dtd 3/18/55, subject, Establishment of a Study Group for Guided Air-to-Air Atomic Rocket. AEC Files, MRA-5, 7/54-6/55, Air-to-Air.

22.

(b)(3)

23.

24. SRD Ltr, Santa Fe Operations Office to Division of Military Application, dtd 4/15/55, subject, Small Atomic Warhead Initially for Use in the High Velocity Unguided Air-to-Air Rocket. AEC Files, MRA-5, 7/54-6/55, Air-to-Air.

25. SRD Report, RS 3466/84406, Air Force Special Weapons Center to Distribution, dtd 4/28/55, subject, Safety Considerations for the XW-25 Air-to-Air Rocket. SC Central Technical Files, XW-25, 1955-61, 2-.

26. SRD Report, RS 3466/84407, Air Force Special Weapons Center to Distribution, dtd 4/28/55, subject, Arming and Fuzing System for the Air-to-Air Atomic Warhead Rocket. Sc Central Technical Files, XW-25, 1955-61, 2-.

27. TSRD Ltr, RS LXI-3132, United States Atomic Energy Commission to Military Liaison Commission, dtd 5/3/55, subject, Development Status. SC Files.

28.

(b)(3)

29. SRD Ltr, Field Command to Sandia Corporation, dtd 5/24/55, subject, Headquarters USAF Logistic Concept, Air-to-Air Atomic Rocket (DING DONG). AEC Files, MRA-5, 7/54-6/55, Air-to-Air.

30. SRD Ltr, Division of Military Application to Santa Fe Operations Office, dtd 6/9/55, subject, XW-25. AEC Files, XW-25, 3/55-6/55.

31. SRD Ltr, RS 1/736, Los Alamos Scientific Laboratory and Sandia Corporation to Santa Fe Operations Office, dtd 8/12/55, subject, Time Scales for XW-25 Production. SC Central Technical Files, XW-25, 1954-61.

32. SRD Minutes, RS 3466/72832, Special Weapons Development Board to Distribution, dtd 8/24/55, subject, Minutes of the 95th Meeting, Part I. SC Archives, Transfer No. 48217.

33.

(b)(3)

34. SRD Ltr, Albuquerque Operations Office to Sandia Corporation, dtd 6/26/56, subject, XW-25 Production Nomenclature. AEC Files, MRA-5, XW-25, 3/56-6/56.

35.

(b)(3)

36. SRD TWX, Air Force Special Weapons Center to Air Research and Development Command, dtd 11/30/56, subject, Possible Delay in AEC W-25 Emergency Capability Commitment. SC Central Technical Files, XW-25, 1954-61.

37. SRD Minutes, RS 3466/87641, Special Weapons Development Board to Distribution, dtd 2/20/57, subject, Minutes of the 105th Meeting, Part I. SC Archives, Transfer No. 48217.

38. SRD Ltr, RS 3466/82852, Air Force Special Weapons Center to Sandia Corporation, dtd 3/29/57. SC Central Technical Files, XW-25/GENIE and DING DONG, 1955-7.

39. SRD Report, RS 3466/26861, Sandia Corporation to Distribution, dtd 8/58, subject, SC4190(TR), Engineering Evaluation of the Mk 25 Mod 0 Warhead. SC Reports Files.

40. SRD Ltr, RS 3466/146700, Albuquerque Operations Office to Sandia Corporation, dtd 1/30/61, subject, ESD Retrofit for Mk 25. SC Central Technical Files, 25 Program, 6-1.

41. SRD Ltr, RS 2300/700, Sandia Corporation to Distribution, dtd 10/4/61, subject, Final Product Change Proposal No. 1355. SC Central Technical Files, Mk 25/LACROSSE, 1960-4.

42. SRD Ltr, RS 3466/79458, Field Command to Los Alamos Scientific Laboratory and Sandia Corporation, dtd 1/12/54, subject, Military Characteristics for Light Weight Multi-Purpose Atomic Warhead. SC Central Technical Files, 30 Program, 1-6.

43.

(b)(3)

44. SRD Ltr, Division of Military Application to Albuquerque Operations Office, dtd 2/28/56, subject, Projects of Questionable Status. AEC Files, MRA-5, 7/55-6/56.

45. SRD Ltr, Assistant Secretary of Defense to United States Atomic Energy Commission, dtd 9/28/54. AEC Files, MRA-5, HONEST JOHN, 7/54.

46. SRD Ltr, Division of Military Application to Albuquerque Operations Office, dtd 4/27/55, subject, Proposed Military Characteristics for an Adaption Kit for the HONEST JOHN, JR. Rocket. AEC Files, MRA-5, HONEST JOHN, 7/54.

47. SRD Ltr, RS 3466/84726, Division of Military Application to Albuquerque Operations Office, dtd 7/13/56, subject, XW-25 Program. SC Central Technical Files, XW-25, 1955-61, 2-.

48. SRD TWX, Albuquerque Operations Office to Division of Military Application, dtd 7/25/56. AEC Files, MRA-5, XW-25, 7/56-11/56.

49.   (b)(3)

50. SRD Ltr, RS 1246/47, Division 1246 to Division 1261, Sandia Corporation, dtd 8/14/56, subject, XW-25 Increased Yield Preliminary Study. SC Central Technical Files, XW-25, 4-.

51.   (b)(3)

52.

53. SRD Report, Joint Feasibility Group to Distribution, dtd 11/9/56, subject, Study Concerning an Atomic Warhead for a Guided Air-to-Air Missile. AEC Files, MRA-5.

54. SRD Ltr, Assistant Secretary of Defense to United States Atomic Energy Commission, dtd 5/27/57. AEC Files, MRA-5, 3/57-6/57.

55.

56.   (b)(3)

57.

www.ingramcontent.com/pod-product-compliance
Lightning Source LLC
Chambersburg PA
CBHW050620110426
42813CB00010B/2626